"In the eighteen pithy essays comprising *Effwords,* Mark Morelli deftly explores the power of words and writing. Riffing on small items such as a broken, abandoned umbrella, a plucked autumn leaf, and a stick tossed into a river, Morelli unveils the rich tapestry of adventure and purpose just below the surface of our ordinary lives. He also declares the communicative nature of jazz the perfect model for dinner conversation, and poses questions after each essay, inviting his readers to continue the conversation. All avid readers — writers, both new and seasoned, as well as teachers, students, and book club members — will find themselves delighted to follow Morelli's lead."

Kimberly Willardson
Editor, *The Vincent Brothers Review*
www.vincentbrothersreview.org

Effwords

essays of

faith, family, fatherhood

& that one, too

BURTENSHAW
MEDIA
Cuyahoga Falls, Ohio

www.markmorelli.net | markemorelli@gmail.com

Chris Graff, Editor/Proofreader | chrisgraffeditor@gmail.com

First Edition, August, 2014

ISBN-13:
978-0615967066

ISBN-10:
061596706X

Burtenshaw Media | 830 Taylor Avenue | Cuyahoga Falls, OH 44221

DEDICATION

For everyone who appears in these essays, anyone who ever encouraged me to write about moments like these, and all who believe that life is lived best as an ongoing conversation, especially William K. Zinnser and the late Sam Cucchiara.

Other books & writing by Mark Morelli at

www.markmorelli.net

B
BURTENSHAW
MEDIA

Burtenshaw Media logo by
Abie McLaughlin Design & Illustration
www.abiemclaughlin.com

Acknowledgments

All of the essays in this book were previously published:

"Wet," *Portage Penny Press*, September, 1992

"Hometown Living: Two Takes," *Vincent Brothers Review*, #19, Vol. VII, No. 3, 2000. A portion of this essay was originally published in 1995 as "My Father's Sons" in *Northern Ohio Live* magazine.

"Keep Up the Good Work," originally published as "My New York City Angel" in *Family Digest*, July/August, 1996

"What Power," *Northern Ohio Live*, August, 1992

"Eff-word," *Active Voice,* March, 1994

"Uncle Don's Kiss," *The Positive Times*, Spring, 1993

"Cinema-verite," *Commonweal*, Nov. 4, 1994

"A Rescue at Sea," *The Net Worker,* April, 1996

"Hurricane Olivia," *Slugfest LTD*, Winter, 1993-94

"Remembrance of Charles Schulz," *Falls News-Press,* Feb. 17, 2000

"Give a Little Whistle," *Friction Magazine*, June 1, 2002

"Dr. Death Rides Again," *The Realist,* September, 1994

"Grow Up," *Active Voice*, July 2000

"He Could No Longer Hold a Broom," originally published as"It is a Privilege to Show Kindness," *Liguorian*, September 1996

"Temp Santa," *Active Voice*, December, 1997

"The Apostledom of Leaves," *National Gardening Magazine*, November/December, 1996

"A Child Finds God through his Handiwork Outside of Church," *The Plain Dealer*, Nov. 11, 2000

Going Places, Who Knows Where," *Vincent Brothers Review*, #20, Vol. VIII, No. 3, 2002

Contents

Wet..1

Hometown Living: Two Takes.......7

Keep Up the Good Work...............24

What Power....................................35

Effword..45

Uncle Tom's Kiss...........................55

Cinema-verite.................................61

A Rescue at Sea..............................69

Hurricane Olivia.............................75

Remembrance of Charles Schulz...85

Give a Little Whistle...................... 91

Dr. Death Rides Again.................. 101

Grow Up...111

He Could No Longer
Hold a Broom..................................119

Temp Santa.....................................127

The Apostledom of Leaves...........141

A Child Finds God through his
Handiwork Outside of Church......147

Going Places,
Who Knows Where........................153

Introduction

These pieces all began as notes impulsively written on scraps of paper. In bank lines. Stop lights. In the margins of grocery lists. Anywhere. They evolved into conversations with myself that grew till they took shape into essays that editors liked enough to publish.

Years passed. I now see that what I explored then are ideas even more important to me today.

Yes, it's gimmicky to entitle this collection *Effwords,* but I believe words count. In thinking about one big word that has lost its value in overuse, I look at the other effwords that represent life's biggest joys, sorrows and conflicts.

When we grapple with these words and the

concepts behind them, we experience the challenges of life and its fullness.

This is me and the pen, wrestling with the profane and the sacred, and trying to figure out which is which.

And the discussion questions I offer you at the end of each essay for further discussion is not to pay tribute to me as a writer but to encourage you as a thinker. The ideas are bigger than me and you. In my writing and in your discussions, we are just the temporary stewards.

EFFWORDS

"There on the grounds of a university, with its high tech centers and think tanks that make for next year's state of the art, I was reminded that there are some contraptions sprung from human ingenuity, and the human will itself, that will always be one-upped by the elements."

Wet

During a break from classes, small college towns belong to a national museum. Each community becomes a still life. The students are gone. They've washed the bar stamps off their hands, stuffed their laundry bags, and headed home to become sons and daughters again. The tall dormitories, the expansive rotundas, the spooky cafeterias empty are as old-time movie lots.

Early one Sunday morning during the break between terms, I strolled on campus. I had it all to myself. No music blared from dorm windows. I overheard no petty complaints about an English paper, a Psych test, or a date who turned out to be a jerk. Black squirrels rustled through the grass and staked claim to the empty parking lots. For once I was privy to the sound of wind and the drizzle was so courteous it nearly missed me. A dozen or so sparrows left their trees and took holiday by an almost empty bag of pretzels. The loud shuffle of the throng was gone, and by myself, I made no more noise than a scratching on the sidewalk. When I walked by, the sparrows didn't even look up. I passed a broken umbrella discarded by a tree. The black tarp was sliced and full of holes, the aluminum spines out of joint, gnarled, bent like the legs of a dead spider.

A scene of defeat. But it was not the umbrella that gave up. It was the umbrella that bore the brunt of the struggle with the wind and rain some nights before. It was a person who gave up the ghost of a chance to stay dry, a person who hopelessly flung the umbrella aside and forged on soaked. There on the grounds of a university, with its high tech centers and think tanks that make for next year's state of the art, I was reminded that there are some contraptions sprung from human ingenuity, and the human will itself, that will always be one-upped by the elements.

We will always get wet.

The Conversation Continues
over coffee and in posts, journals,
books clubs and classrooms.

Take a brief walk around your home, or any space
you work or dwell. What small item – possibly
even discarded – tells a bigger story?

Complete this statement using another word. "We
will always _____." Then tell the story that
illustrates it.

Reflect upon a moment when you recognized that
forces were bigger than you.

"The gravest folly of all is to let yourself go untraveled in all ways, to let dust settle on both your books and your boots."

Hometown Living: Two Takes
Take 1: Notes on Home
Written in Ohio, 1994. Revised in New York City, 1999.

I grew up in a small town, but I moved away.
My eldest brother stayed. He is a pillar of the
community. I always had wanderlust. He never
did, or at least never indulged it.

I've had fifteen addresses. I can easily
remember only the one I have now and the
one where I grew up, where my parents still live.
I've watched seals flop around in the icy, salty
Piscataqua River that separates Maine from New
Hampshire. I've seen the sun rise over the East
River from a rooftop on the Lower East Side of
Manhattan. I've sold fireworks and gotten a boss
tan from the back of a truck in Daytona Beach.
I've strummed guitar and yodeled into great
hillsides along New York State Route 17, caring

7

not a whit that it was 3am and my alternator was dead.

My brother, on the other hand, lives two blocks from our parents' home and his children are blessed with grandparents they know intimately. He is active in our hometown church and has served as the Water Board Commissioner for years. Diligently, he has spearheaded the necessary changes to bring the community's water system up to standard while the systems in neighboring towns remain antiquated and costly to operate. He plays cards with friends he has known since kindergarten.

When I'm in town, we take long walks together. People nod and give him a nonchalant hello. To me, they react with surprise. I'm a visitor now, not a resident. I am, so to speak, news. Of course, the out-of-towner no longer brings in tales from the outside. What I bring is not information; instead, I am the embodiment of perspective. I've been away.

"Hey, where have you been? Where are you living now? It's good to see you, don't be a stranger."

I treasure their friendliness, but honestly, I don't deserve it heaped so high. If anyone does, it's my brother. What have I done to shape their lives? It is he who has done nothing less than ensure their children safe drinking water. Hail not the conquering hero, but the one who stayed.

The allure lies in what's just over the horizon. In Sherwood Anderson's timeless 1919 novel *Winesburg, Ohio*, George Willard, the young man who writes the town's newspaper, burns with desire to see the world, write great things, love beautiful women. He seeks the fountain of aspirations where he might hold his empty decanter. He has not yet reached the age that Cleveland poet Stanley Niemiec depicts in "Old Men":

Unlike the young they have learned
That life is not always sweet,
That ambition and accomplishment
Seldom meet.

Winesburg, Ohio concludes on a railroad platform, with George Willard heading to the big city, looking at his hometown as a "background on which to paint the dreams of his manhood." We don't know what becomes of George Willard. He might've returned home, living the words of George Moore: "A man travels the world over in search of what he needs, and returns home to find it." After all, only a fool persists in thinking he can get close enough to the horizon to plant a flag in it.

10

Another George in our cultural imagination is George Bailey, the dreamer who could never unshackle himself from his father's obligations in Frank Capra's 1946 film "It's A Wonderful Life." George Bailey never made it to the train platform, and stuck with the burdens of his father's business, is driven to the brink of suicide. When his dreams of travel and adventure slowly curdled into a life of inadvertent scandal and financial ruin, life was not worth living. He finally triumphed, as everyone knows, by realizing that life is the journey itself, not the destination.

Smalltowners forget that city dwellers are often more provincial because they are in awe of no one and no place. Big cities are nothing but compartmentalized neighborhoods. E.B. White wrote that "people from villages and small towns, people accustomed to the convenience and friendliness of neighborhood over-the-fence living, are unaware that life in New York follows the neighborhood pattern."

New York has changed since E.B. White's day, but his observations on urban life ring true enough. When the May Company announced last year [1993] that it would close its huge downtown Cleveland store, Richard Osborne, editor of *Corporate Cleveland* magazine, lamented the passing of other businesses, some born locally, such as Higbee's, Halle's, Sterling's, Richman's, Sohio, Hough Bakeries and the old Cleveland Trust. Osborne wrote:

Businesses are truly successful not merely when they make money, but when they make memories, too. And then they expand the community's definition of itself. The names belonged to us uniquely – which of course may be one of the reasons they are gone. But while we had them, they gave our town a flavor and texture all its own.

12

And they made us proud.

Likewise, I feel a pang when I stroll my childhood small town neighborhood and pass the corner building that was, long ago, a candy store. It was run by an old English couple named Burgess who sold penny root beer barrels and Popsicles. Shopping there between five and six meant you interrupted their dinner. This contributed to the flavor and texture of my neighborhood in a way that a chain convenience store never could. Then again, I could be wrong. Every childhood creates its own memories.

So no matter where we go, we will always be somewhere else unless we come to fully know that flavor and texture that is the town's very own. Transients, despite whatever worldliness they gain, will never know a town so well.

Yet, we provincials still long for cities. And though time has taught me that people are the same everywhere, the energies of the city still make my heart thump. When from a bus, train or car, I come within view of a skyline, particularly Manhattan's, I shiver with delight.

While riding the Staten Island Fairy, I overheard a man who lived in New York showing his out-of-town nephew the grandeur of lower Manhattan's skyline. I envied him and lamented that I wasn't a native New Yorker, that I didn't have such grand vistas to show off. But once I thought about it, I also had such an experience.

When my own nephew was ten, I showed him an old doorstep in the one-block business district of our small Ohio hometown. In the early 1900s, this stoop led into an ice cream parlor. Long ago, a mason had laid the colored tile on the stoops to read *Ice Cream and Candy*. My nephew hadn't noticed the words before. Few people do anymore. The ice cream and candy store had been replaced fifty years before. On our next walk, he stopped and showed the tiled words of the long ago confection store to one of his buddies. Together they shared a slice of history about their town and I put no small value on that knowledge. That nephew is part of the fourth generation to live in our hometown since his great-grandfather came from Italy in 1900. He is the fourth to carry our surname. So when our name is mentioned, it resounds with local history. My nephew is part of a continuing chain, a continuity. He walks the same sidewalks as his immigrant great-grandfather, his grandfather and his father. He might feel good, being part of something, a link in the chain. On the other hand, he might feel the sentiment of Paul Simon: "In my little town, I never meant nothing, I was just my father's son," and a desire to break the chain. After all, his great-grandfather broke a much longer chain by way of Ellis Island.

Shortly after graduating from college, I abruptly quit my radio job in Youngstown to move to New England, not for another job or school, but just to go, to live near the sea. It was my first time living outside of Ohio. But now I realize that it wasn't by any means my first journey. As a boy, nestled in my bedroom, I would read book after book. I could hear the trains roar through our village at night, but it was the quiet turning of pages that sent me far afield. To commune with authors across a vast space has turned out to be even more important than physical travel because

16

it has taught me to venture always and everywhere, to make a journey of watching a bird feed its young, a spider spin its web, a stranger on a ferry pointing out a skyline, or showing a young boy an old stoop. The gravest folly of all is to let yourself go untraveled in all ways, to let dust settle on both your books and your boots.

Take 2: Back Home From NYC, 2000

I drove up the Howard Street hill from downtown Akron and glanced into the rear-view mirror.

Never before had the Akron skyline reminded me of New York's and those of you who have laid eyes on both know that it never will.

There's no comparison.

But this time, probably because it was framed like a closely cropped postcard in my tiny car mirror, the Akron skyline looked stunning, if only for a few seconds.

Why did this image stick with me? Why do I even need to be reminded of New York?

Because I sorely miss metropolitan life.

And if not metropolitan life, then its promise. New York is the city of possibilities. Difficulties. Luck. Failure. If I can make there. That skyline, that fabulous, breath-taking, awe-inspiring, exhausting New York City skyline. The numbing, exhilarating, full-of-promise-and-potential city of stories. Maybe my story.

Well, my *short* story since I am now already back in my native Ohio, and pretty much glad to be back, even though there is much I miss about New York. But I left it. I could not get it under my thumb. Unconquerable, it spit me out.

Yet not before I had a few jobs, viewing the

city at lunch through my high-rise office, taking comedy writing classes, walking the length of Broadway, seeing shows, going elbow to elbow in subways, nodding off on buses, basking in the relaxing river of human energy of Central Park on Sunday afternoons, and the most surprising thrill of all – giving directions to tourists.

I often forget the grueling aspect of it. I remember the romance like I fondly remember an old girlfriend – with whom I was incompatible and who became someone else's bride – every time I get a passing whiff of White Linen.

I take daily walks around downtown Akron where I capture weak but sufficient reminders of my glorious lunchtime walks in Manhattan. But step into any downtown Akron office building and look at the ledger on the lobby wall. Law firms, government offices, social services – it all seemed the same in every building. Where was the diversity? All the colorful start-ups and dotcoms? I made the ridiculous mistake of trying to unfairly compare anything to New York. Downtown Akron has no Carnegie Deli. Why should it?

The mystic poet Rumi said, "If you've not been fed, be bread." After leaving New York, I should stop feeling entitled to anything more spectacular than I can build myself. Trees jutting from hillsides bend their trunks toward the sun.

Color with the crayons you have. And so I color. But how do you go from 64 colors to 8, half of them broken? How can I find the vivacity of the never-to-be-duplicated city now that I am back in Ohio?

I don't have the right answer, but I'm beginning to weed out the wrong ones. And one that is definitely off the mark is my mistaking New York

City as the only incubator for the magic human creativity that I seek.

And a chance glance in the rear-view mirror should fuel my inspiration, not my regrets. There is something to be said for where I've been. It has lead me to here.

I will be bread.

The Conversation Continues
over coffee and in posts, journals, books clubs and classrooms.

What has led you to where you are today?

What has disappointment taught you?

What have you shown – or would you show – to younger people you know to help them better understand themselves and their heritage?

"Keep up the good work.

Let your light shine."

-Monsignor Toohy keeping alive Matthew 5:16

Keep Up the Good Work

I had recently moved to New York City. I was so eager to sample the variety of New York churches that I attended Mass at a different parish every Sunday. That particular week I chose the church of the Blessed Sacrament on West 71st , more than 50 blocks away from my small downtown sublet. Like countless other older Catholic churches in New York, it had a high cathedral ceiling, ornate columns, brilliant classical murals and statues, and is rarely filled to capacity. On previous Sundays, I observed mostly Italian names etched on stained glass windows in Little Italy and Greenwich Village, strong Italian neighborhoods during the first half of this century. But here on the Upper West Side, these names were mostly Irish.

During these Masses, I sought strength to

remain rooted in faith, to patiently persevere in my job hunt despite the deep longing I felt for my wife and daughter. They were still back home in our native Ohio, where I had spent the last two years teaching part-time at a community college while looking for a full-time job. After dozens of interviews and heartbreaking near misses and close calls, I came up empty-handed and dejected.

During these two years, our first child was born. I thought to myself, "How can I teach my child to pursue her own dreams if I don't pursue my own?" I always wanted to tackle New York, but I spent too many years dawdling, trying different things – teaching, newspaper reporting, radio announcing.

I was already married and a father with responsibilities, a bit behind in the ideal time to make a go of it in New York.

There is hardly a job worse than the task of finding a job. And in New York, where verve and tenacity are bare minimum requirements, the job hunt can be bitter and grueling. E.B. White observed that the city "can destroy an individual, or it can fulfill him, depending a good deal on luck. No one should come to New York to live unless he is willing to be lucky." Although I believed in my talent, I felt more desperate than lucky, and I was praying for good luck, strength and some days, just a bounce in my step.

So each week at these different churches, I asked for strength to keep seeking a home for my talents. Then I prayed for faith, that with hard work and good conscience, my work and talents would come to some good.

After Mass, I sat for awhile to collect my thoughts. Still, I was discouraged. Almost everyone exited the church. In the back of the church, a tall priest spoke with two little old ladies. I paid them no notice and walked through the open doors. The priest suddenly was on the outside steps with me.

"Keep up the good work," he said to me.

I turned around and looked at him. He faced me. *What an unusual thing to say.* Perplexed, I stepped toward him. He was not even the priest who had just officiated the service. He said goodbye to the old ladies and came closer to me, looking intently but kindly.

"Hello," I said, squinting into the spring sun. "Nice day."

He agreed. I told him how I had been to many other churches and noticed that this one, by the inscriptions of donor names on the walls near the stained glass windows, looked like it had a history of Irish parishioners.

"We've had all kinds," he said. "At one time, this was a very wealthy neighborhood. That's all changed."

"These big churches don't fill up these days," I said.

"I think that's because when these churches were built, we did not have evening and Saturday Masses," the priest said.

"I see," I said. "I like a packed house. There seems to be more power. Like when you wrap a bundle of sticks and they seem stronger, harder to break than if the sticks were singular and more fragile."

"Yes," he said. "Now the people seem to be more spread out. This church used to have six thousand people attending every Sunday. We had to offer a 6 a.m. Mass in the old days."

"Old days?" You don't seem that old."

"I've been here off and on for 30 years. This was my first assignment after I was ordained. What's your name?"

"Mark."

"Glad to meet you, Mark. I'm Monsignor Toohy. T-O-O-H-Y. That's Irish."

"Well, Monsignor, this is a beautiful church."

"It's French architecture," he said, adding that it was modeled after Sainte Chappelle, a 14th century Gothic church in Paris.

"Father Toohy, you know something? Yours was the first smile I received this morning. Oops, I called you Father. I mean Monsignor."

"I'm still a priest," he said in amusement. "Your first smile, eh? Think about it. Only human beings can smile. It's a divine gift."

I was still preoccupied by his initial

29

comment. *Keep up the good work.* Was I reading too much into it? How did he know it was the exact affirmation that I needed?

Our conversation never went past small talk. I never told him that I was despondent and tired in my job hunt. I never mentioned that I was away from my wife and daughter. I didn't say how I was on pins and needles awaiting answers from all my job leads and application letters, and how after two years of wavering between part-time and full-time and back to part-time employment, I was sick and tired of the whole process. I said none of this.

His smile put me at ease. For the first time, I felt like I was doing good work, and I ought to keep it up. "Have a good day, Monsignor Toohy," I said and walked down the steps and onto the sidewalk.

He didn't say "goodbye" or "take care." He

didn't say "come back again" or even "God bless you." Instead he said, "Keep up the good work, Mark. Let your light shine." I walked halfway down the block before I looked back. Monsignor Toohy was gone. I took a deep breath and stood in my tracks.

A little later at a coffee shop, I tried reading the Sunday *Times* classifieds. But my mind was back on those church steps. I wondered if perhaps there was no Monsignor Toohy. Maybe he didn't exist. Maybe he was an angel. I pulled the church bulletin from my back pocket. Sure enough, Monsignor Toohy's name was listed near the masthead. I didn't care. I decided he was still an angel.

Note: William J. Rev. Monsignor William J.
Toohy, of Blessed Sacrament Parish in Manhattan

died June 12, 2011 at age 80. My late friend, the publisher, teacher and writer Sam Cucchiara, loved this essay and adopted the Monsignor's words, "Keep up the good work, let your light shine," as he signed off his many letters to me and others. My one encounter with Monsignor Toohy, and my fifteen-year friendship with Sam Cucchiara, illustrate the power each of us has to affirm others, whether we meet for just a moment or countless times. I continue to sign off many of my letters in that same way.

The Conversation Continues
over coffee and in posts, journals,
books clubs and classrooms.

*Reflect upon how someone's encouragement – or
lack of it – has affected your life.*

*Ponder and discuss how your encouragement – or
lack of it – has affected others' lives.*

*Remember when you met someone just once, even
a stranger, who said something to you that you
will never forget.*

*What would you like your "sign off" – the way you
say goodbye to people – to be?*

"Today we have a plethora of distractions, which keep us from thinking long about any one thing."

And I wrote this *before* the emergence of the internet and social.

                   -mm, 2014, 20 years later

What Power

After years of mowing lawns, I took my first payroll job at age sixteen and learned how people interpret the U.S. Constitution. I was a pizza baker. The young woman who prepared the pizza dough with sauce, cheese and other toppings was the only other worker on my shift. Missy was a married teenager who lived in the upstairs of a close-to-rickety farmhouse. She and her husband, who brought her to work on an old, rattling Harley, didn't have two nickels to rub together. The man who owned the farmhouse lived downstairs.

Missy talked and talked while I baked and baked. One night she said, "My landlord complains when I play my stereo. Last night he said, 'It's too loud.' I said, 'I have every right to play my music as loud as I want. It's my freedom of expression.' Then he said, 'No, Missy, you've got that wrong. Freedom of expression is your right to turn that crap down and try to convince me that you ought to be allowed to turn it up loud again.'"

Missy snorted in disbelief and plopped down the ground sausage. "Can you imagine someone bitchin' so much about Led Zeppelin?"

Fifteen years after Missy's brush with the rock 'n roll Gestapo, I stood in front of a college classroom where nineteen incurious but polite young people pretended to listen to me while two actually did. I know this because I got a rise out of them when I said, "Not everyone has a right to free speech. If you aren't prepared to back up what you say or work hard enough to understand why you think the way you do, then your right has as much value as last year's calendar and you may as well forget it."

"No!" the two responded in an outrage that was still subdued not to disturb the daydreamers.

Good, I thought. Even a two out of twenty-one response rate is a decent return on my investment, and quite a trick when you think that the 19 others never even woke up.

But it is getting harder for people to find time and space to think. I subscribe to *The New Yorker*, a weekly magazine that can easily pile up unread. A newspaper editor friend remarked, "*The New Yorker* was made for a time when there was nothing else fun to do at home but listen to the radio." Today, we have a plethora of distractions, which keeps us from thinking long about any one thing. We are unaccustomed to slowness. We need an opinion *now*, because the poll questions change tomorrow.

We like snappy answers. We want our politicians self-assured and quick (but perhaps not too slick.) Once, on a radio talk show, I heard a caller berate a politician for taking too long to answer. "I have to think before I talk, ma'am," he said with a weird apology. On another radio talk show, I heard an old man say, concerning a new legislative proposal, "Well, I don't know anything about that, but I'm against it!"

Judgmental audience members of television talk shows of the *Jerry Springer* ilk gluttonously ravage the poor souls onstage – who are gluttons themselves – giving thumbs up and thumbs down like a cranky, hungover Roman mob at the gladiatorial matches. One morning, I was in a hospital waiting room, and on the intrusive television Montel Williams was interviewing relatives of slain hookers. Here's what we saw:

From audience to guests, back and forth, people said cruel and distasteful things to each other. Complete strangers formed opinions of each other faster than it takes a tear to drop, all mouths and no ears, venting empty fury on each other and us viewers. It was so annoying that I stood up and turned it off. A few people in the waiting room sighed with relief. "I feel better already," an old man joked to his wife. "Can we go home now?"

I'd seen empty fury a few years earlier in college. There was a bar on campus called the Rathskeller. Thursdays were "Alternative Night" which meant the deejay played songs one wouldn't normally hear on the radio. It attracted kids who wore black leather, army boots, torn shirts, nose rings and spiked hair.

As I walked past the bar after my evening class, one of the kids snarled to my back. "That's right, we're wearing black!" He raised his fist triumphantly. That's it. He had spoken.

"And...?" I said, but there was nothing left for him to say. Beneath the leather and safety pins was a frustrated soul. He reminded me of the title of a Harlan Ellison book, *I Have No Mouth and I Must Scream.*

Our brains teem and swirl with thoughts but we all do something different with that flow. It would be good to channel it through the generators of reason, inquiry and imagination into well-formed ideas. Too often, it just gets caught on the rocks and goes nowhere.

A friend of mine, who is seventy-seven years old, laments the passing of cheek-to-cheek dancing. "When I was young, I'd practice with my date all week. On Saturday nights, we had a chemistry. It was real satisfying because we had mastered the steps, danced out all the kinks during the week in my garage. Now, there's no need to practice. There are no steps."

Dancing can be a metaphor for thinking and expression. For just as the tango, a difficult dance, is seductive and powerful, one who can shape ideas with words can have power over life and not resort to wearing black and screaming or claiming that the founding fathers were all about the volume of Led Zeppelin.

Imagine the power of presenting one's ideas with the rhythm of a practiced waltz, instead of thinking and speaking always in a slam-dance rage.

What power – to say exactly what one wants to say. It is our constitutional right to *cultivate* that power to express ourselves, lucidly and precisely and persuasively. In this world of way too much information, we are often estranged not only from our loved ones and neighbors, but from our own thoughts. What power, to cut through all the phone wires and satellite beams and pulsating radios and allow our thoughts take root long enough to understand them. Then nurture them so that others can understand them, too. How many children would not go astray, how many marriages would be saved, how many satisfying careers launched, how many estranged families reconnected, if people would only respect that power to think slowly and certainly, to hold back the jerking knee, and stiff-arm this week's lusty pollsters.

The Conversation Continues
over coffee and in posts, journals, books clubs
and classrooms.

*How has your ability to communicate served you
well – or failed you?*

*Who impresses you with the way they use their
words?*

*Does social media keep us connected...or quash
conversation?*

"*Omit needless words* asserts Strunk and White in their classic writing guide, *Elements of Style.* And the effword has become needless. Not because it is vulgar, but because its obscenity, its only usefulness, has been worn out. Its overuse has worn out its springs to become as useless as a droopy trampoline."

Effword

I take strolls across the campus with Stephanie, a fellow writing teacher. She's a generation ahead of me – a girl who grew up in wartime England with all the Keep Calm and Carry On strength and reserve of that generation in that place.

She is stately and prim but never stuffy, as uniform as her slacks are creased. Her hair is bobbed like a silver bell. She chooses her words carefully and her language is both colorful and concise.

Stephanie and I talk about literature, students' papers, television, magazines, pets, my child, her grandchildren, politics, or the best place in town for pancakes.

One day, two clean cut college boys spun by on bicycles.

"Where the fuck we having dinner?" one said to the other in a calm, vanilla voice.

Stephanie halted. She turned her neck like an owl, watching the boys ride by.

"Do you think they *saw* me here?" she asked, more puzzled than offended.

"Sure."

"And they said that word." She shook her head, not in shock, but in wonder of the changing times.

"Young people use it all the time, like it's air," I said.

"I certainly am a relic," she said. "That word used to really mean something. You know, it's not even that vulgar to *me* anymore. What *does* it mean now?"

"Omit needless words," asserts Strunk and

White in their classic writing guide, *Elements of Style*. And the effword has become needless. Not because it is vulgar, but because its obscenity – its only usefulness – has been worn out. Its overuse has worn out its springs to become as useless as a droopy trampoline.

Even a flasher at a ladies' card club will eventually become part of the scenery, making themselves useful by passing out finger sandwiches and loading the dishwashers as the card party resumes. Strunk and White also state that "Vigorous writing is concise." An expletive's purpose is to add vigor to language, to set it ablaze, but the effword now does the opposite, making language imprecise, clumsy, too soggy to catch fire.

When I was a little boy in the sixties and

seventies, the effword still packed gunpowder. It was dangerous to play with, uttered as a last resort, never within the earshot of adults. You never heard it on television. My parents (come now!) never said it. It wasn't spoken in the homes in our neighborhood, at least not in front of children. I suppose if you were in the habit of saying it, you left it at the door like a gentleman leaves his hat.

On Thursdays, the day my mother got out of the house to go bowling, I'd listen to my older brothers' records: George Carlin, the songs from *Hair* and *Woodstock*, and old Redd Foxx party albums. I didn't want anyone catching me, so I locked the doors, put on my brothers' puffy earmuff-sized headphones, and listened to all this juicy, dirty language like a war orphan whose heart pounds after swiping a pack of Camels.

Woodstock gave us Country Joe McDonald's

Fish Cheer, a big dumb hulking effword chant that meant to shock. It was clunky, not clever, but it wasn't meant to give Noel Coward a run for his money. It was meant to shock, which it did, because in 1969, the effword was still filthy. Country Joe was trying to smear grime onto the white tablecloth that was still American mass media.

Today [this essay was originally published in 1994] the spigot of profanity in conversation, TV and music is wrenched open and the bilge gushes directly into our homes and public places. By its very preponderance, foul language ceases even to be *foul* anymore. In *The Atlantic Monthly*, Francis Davis points out rap's "monotonous profanity," and such monotony is an affront to those who value language. In music, the unexpected note perks up the ear. A tune with just one note is not a tune at all.

In a college writing class I took ten years ago, a prim young woman attempted to lend intensity to her short story so she slathered the dialogue with the effword. Our teacher kindly asked why.

"I want it to be rough and realistic," she explained, not a little desperately. If profanity is dashed into dialogue like a spice, what she gave us was a bushel full of pepper, overpowering and unpalatable. A ruined dish.

The effword, like fireworks, will wow a crowd only on special occasions. Done all the time, it will keep us awake on a work night.

It wasn't always like this. In 1946, it reared its head slyly, when Norman Mailer had to spell it *fugging* in his novel *The Naked and the Dead.* When saucy actress Tallulah Bankhead met the up-and-coming author she said, "Oh yes, you're the young man who doesn't know how to spell fuck."

I teach college English. I give the Effword Lecture. I write it on the board, big as Hollywood, then describe everything in the room using that adjective. "The word is used incorrectly because no sex is taking place in the room."

"That I know of," I add for laughs.

"Also, its use as an expletive is inappropriate since I'm expressing no rage. And finally, the word doesn't have its old shock value kick anymore. To quote Constant Lambert, 'It is clear that we are fast losing even the minor stimulus of genuine healthy vulgarity.'"

Eff-this and eff-that signifies laziness. It is the cook who is too hurried and lazy to cut the lard from the fat-spackled brisket. The effword takes up space, adds to the heft, but provides no nutrition.

It is mental surrender. Once all points and counterpoints are exhausted, it is eff-you, back and forth. Then, at least here in America, gunfire.

Stephanie and I and all the other writing teachers are not a legion of linguistic Carrie Nations*. We are not barging into pool halls, buttoning lips. We are not on any blue-lipped crusade to wipe out the effword. We just believe that words are tools for sculpting, even stabbing. But a dull tool does neither.

I leave you with this recommendation on how to save the effword: Preserve it's shock value. Use it with the frequency that you would go up and kiss a stranger.

*Carrie Nation (1846-1911) led the Woman's Christian Temperance Union. She was known for entering saloons and attacking stills and barrels with a hatchet.

The Conversation Continues
over coffee and in posts, journals, books clubs and classrooms.

Where are you on this: It's no big deal or it's
offensive?

Is it just natural and courteous – or is it phony – to
change your vocabulary around certain people?
Should there be words – topics, even – that
children shouldn't hear?

This essay led to the book's title. What do those
other *effwords mean to you?*

"They had not seen him as we last did, gathering up every last bit of energy he had left to give his wife a small kiss."

Uncle Tom's Kiss

My wife and I went to visit my Aunt Amy to keep her company because she lived alone. She was a widow of the worst kind. Her husband still lived. She was 85 and he was a few years younger. He lived in a nearby nursing home. The man who had stood tall and handsome, with curly snowy hair, a Clark Gable mustache and a zest for living, was now in bed, twisted and sick, his mind far away.

Uncle Tom had suffered successive strokes, each one stripping away bit by bit his power to speak, but none strong enough to overcome his will to live.

Aunt Amy never complained. She found rides twice a day to see him, bringing cookies and cups of pudding. Perhaps in the quiet of her privacy she grieved, but in public, she kept her chin up and even boasted that Uncle Tom still had his legendary appetite.

At the nursing home, she fed Uncle Tom from his tray of soft vegetables and tiny bits of meat. She wiped his chin but never talked to him like he was a baby. After more than fifty years of marriage you don't baby talk your husband. You yell like a wife.

"Tom, eat this! Don't make such a mess Look who came to visit you," she said with volume, but love.

I'd heard that voice all my life. Before, it was "Take off your boots" or "Shut off the mower and have lunch" or "Get those tools off the table." Back then, Uncle Tom would comply but laugh.

But Aunt Amy never stopped trying to make him respond. Month after month, after two years, her sturdy carpenter husband didn't say anything back, but she never gave up.

I was puzzled. Were my uncle's thought

sealed inside him and unable to get out? Or had they, like a raft on a gushing river, been cut free and left to float away forever? Was he trapped, constantly and tirelessly treading water in his own pool of thought, or just there, a heartbeat wrapped in skin?

It was time to leave the nursing home. My wife and I said goodbye to my uncle in his wheelchair. We were uncertain whether he even recognized us or understood our words.

A moment later our uncertainty was gone. My aunt leaned over him. "Goodbye," she said. "Give me a kiss."

His eyes were still vacant and distant, his body motionless, but he stretched his weak neck forward and puckered his lips.

A few weeks later he died. At his funeral, people who hadn't seen him in years were shocked at what had become of the strong, tireless man they once knew. They had not seen him as we last did, gathering up every last bit of energy he had left to give his wife a small kiss.

What an amazing moment. I learned that the barriers made by strokes and heart attacks, things that can afflict a mind and body, are still no match for the power of love and the promises we make in its name.

The Conversation Continues
over coffee and in posts, journals, books clubs and classrooms.

Whose positive spirit to you admire?

If love is disposable, is it really love?

Write or talk about the deeper meaning of these phrases: Thick or thin. Better or worse. Rain or shine. Cut your losses. Good money after bad. Know when to quit. A promise is a promise.

About this essay

Remember when it was a whole new way of life to watch complete movies at home with no commercials?

Readers born after 1985, pull up an apple crate and listen to this tale from a bygone era.

P.S. I have evolved and am now at peace with video on demand.

-mm, 2014

Cinema-verite

I liked it when the movie theater was the only place to see movies. I went enthusiastically, even if the movie was mediocre. It was good to get out. In *Annie Hall*, Diane Keaton thinks it's great to watch movies in a home screening room (the mansion of the producer played by Paul Simon.) But Woody disagrees. It isn't the same if you don't "make the effort" of going out to the theater.

Now we have VCRs. For a measly dollar I can see a movie in my home without combing my hair or putting on shoes. If the movie falls short of phenomenal, I walk out of the room with indifference. Worse, if I find the movie phenomenal, I am still indifferent, scratching my belly at the fridge. There's no thrill of "making the effort" and meeting the artist halfway. I don't exit onto a sidewalk. There are no bright lights or drinks afterward, or the chance of running into an old friend in the lobby. Watching movies at home has become like the fifth Apollo moonwalk. Blase.

For a few years I would encounter a mysterious guy in a trench coat in the lobby of the Uptown Theater in Youngstown after a foreign flick. Sounds creepy, I know, but here's what happened. We'd launch into discussions about the film. After fifteen minutes of enjoyably pedantic discussion, we would both turn heel and go separate ways. I never knew his name. A rewarding intellectual experience in public. No doubt, a frightening one had it happened in my home.

It took my wife and I three days to watch *JFK* because we paused to finish laundry, answer the phone, feed the baby, throw in some more laundry, all hacking at the film's continuity. I only listened to *What About Bob?* but later told people I saw it, which is like smelling a 46-oz. steak but demanding a trophy for having eaten it as well. I hated *Heathers* because I thought it was too much of everything: horror story, after-school special, black comedy, romance. While my wife tried to watch it, I wouldn't shut up with my dime-store criticism. In the theater, I wouldn't have said a word, just behaved myself, and let the movie play. It would have been all over in two hours.

As a teen movie buff in the seventies I scoured *TV Guide* for old films. Loud car salesmen in big bow ties couldn't deter me from fighting sleep to see Boris Karloff, Lionel Barrymore, Clark Gable and Abbott & Costello. These films often aired in the middle of the night. Where now I set my VCR, then I set my alarm. Yawning, rubbing my squeaking eyes, I watched the movies. I made the effort.

I'd also rise at 6:30 on Saturday mornings to watch a film series of classic comedies that were edited to one hour. The choppy editing didn't bother me. I was thrilled that I happened to be there to see them. I met Laurel & Hardy, Wheeler & Woolsey, the Marx Brothers, Red Skelton, and a sharper, hilarious Bob Hope I'd not seen on his TV specials. Not because I "rented" the movies at my convenience, but because our paths crossed. It was serendipity. It was my good luck. Who knew then, highlighting the *TV Guide* or waiting for the film to arrive at our local theater, that I'd have the choice of *thousands* of films, and hate it. Thousands is too much, like a mile-long buffet when I just want scrambled eggs.

You should see us at our local video store. I want to see an old Jerry Lewis, but my wife likes *Beaches.* I'm looking at the Marx Brothers, but she sniffs disapproval. I'm in the mood for a comedy when she's in the mood for a warm drama. She's feels like a comedy and I feel like a foreign film.

I'm always, and she is never, up for a World War II documentary.

We can settle for a Hitchcock. You can't miss with Hitchcock. But Hitchcocks, like the sands of time, are running out.

One time we roamed indecisively from shelf to shelf. The longer we stayed, reading the copy on the tape cases, the more it became a chore. We spent an hour trying to decide how to spend the next two hours. Then we looked out the window into the parking lot. A burly man in an overcoat turned up his collar and forged through the falling snow toward his lonely Impala at the far end of the lot.

"He's slipping," my wife said.

"I hope he makes it," I said.

He slipped and slid, looking silly but at least keeping his balance until he was just ten feet from his car. "Almost," I said. But he fell, spinning on his bottom like Donald O'Connor.

"Think he's hurt?" my wife wondered. With the doggedness of Oliver Hardy, he shook the snow from his coat, tugged his hat, and with dignity salvaged, strode the rest of the way to his car.

We cheered. "He made it!"

The snow could have melted off his hot neck. He revved his engine. The headlights, like great spotlights, made a beauty shot of the thick, ornate snowflakes, which scattered in the cold wind like chorus girls in a Busby Berkeley spectacular.

"Wow," I said.

"Beautiful," she said.

"Coffee?" I suggested.

"Sure."

We left empty handed.

The Conversation Continues
over coffee and in posts, journals, books clubs and classrooms.

When are fewer choices better?

How does being entertained at home differ from being entertained in public?

Do you people watch? What do you see?

"With that friendship, Mike put into practice every good faith lesson he'd ever heard."

A Rescue at Sea

They had been adrift on that flimsy boat in the South China Sea for too many days to even guess. Some died. They were starving and parched. Boats passed them by, ignoring their cries for help. There were sixty-three boat people trying to escape cruelty, who had each paid five hundred to a thousand dollars for boat passage out of Vietnam. They now faced the ultimate cruelty of being stranded to die at sea.

Then they came within sight of another boat. With their last gasps of energy, under the baking sun, they cried out.

"Save us!"

"Help me!"

"We will all die!"

These were the words written down in the deck logbook of the M/V Rover, manned by the Seafarers in the Government Service Division

(Merchant Marine), after rescuing the refugees. Mike Maxwell, the chief cook, prepared the gentle foods that the refugees slowly put into their raw, shrunken stomachs.

This was just over ten years ago. [This essay was published in 1996.] The story could end there and still be a happy one.

Thai Minh-Tran, a 26-year-old Vietnamese seminarian, was glad to be alive. But Thai, who had no friends or relatives in the states to sponsor him, was returned to Vietnam. His hopes to escape darkened.

Until he was befriended by the man who had prepared the food that brought him back to life. With that friendship, Mike Maxwell put into practice every good faith lesson he'd ever heard. And he pledged not only his own, but the friendship of his family in New Jersey.

Mike's father contacted Catholic Social

Services in Newark, who helped them through the application process but were very pessimistic about Thai's chances of getting to America.

The Maxwells contacted a priest in Gretna, Louisiana who had been one of Thai's teachers in Vietnam. This priest enlisted the aid of his order, the Blessed Sacred Congregation. Thai was admitted to the U.S. as a seminarian with a new language and culture.

Mike helped Thai learn about this country. He traveled to Gretna and took Thai for a long tour of the U.S. – Houston, Los Angeles, San José, San Francisco, Reno, Chicago, Cleveland and finally back to the family's home in River Edge, New Jersey.

On April 16, 1994, the Maxwells attended Thai's ordination at Corpus Christi Church in Houston.

There, Thai gave back to Mike the bread of life.

The Conversation Continues
over coffee and in posts, journals,
books clubs and classrooms.

*Who came to your rescue in a moment of
desperation?*

*Who have you helped in their moment of
desperation?*

*Discuss a time when you encountered somebody at
exactly the right moment.*

Who in your life, besides an old college roommate with the power to blackmail you, has the license to call at 4:15 a.m. and scream into the phone, *Waaah! I'm hungry! Bring me something to eat!...*?

Hurricane Olivia

In 1969, gulf Florida residents braced for Hurricane Camille. Newspapers printed warnings. Radio and TV reports frantically urged all to take cover. Most did. But there was a defiant group of people in a beachfront mansion who fancied themselves immortal. They chose to greet the storm with a party. Fortified by martinis, they stood outside and raised their glasses to Hurricane Camille, as if she would turn heel when mocked. But Camille showed up – and how – and some of the brazen decadents didn't make it out alive.

With all due respect to those who perished in that real storm, that story is how I'd describe the birth of our first child, Olivia Rose. We knew it was coming, but we didn't take cover. We were warned a thousand times, but we were not only unprepared for the abrupt change that slammed into us, we had stuck our tongues out at it.

The first abrupt change happened immediately. It detonated like a bomb. Something happened to us that we hadn't experienced since our undergraduate days: Screaming in the middle of the night.

We wondered, who is this little screaming epidermal pod, daring to wake us so rudely in the middle of the night? Not even your dearest friends have permission to do that. Who in your life, besides an old college roommate with the power to blackmail you, has the license to call at 4:15 a.m. and scream into the phone, *Waaah! I'm hungry! Bring me something to eat!...?*

And college is what I'd been thinking of all along during my wife's pregnancy. I just assumed she would be giving birth to a bright little 19-year-old who would visit me on weekends for three hour coffees and discussions about books and music and love. What was all this screaming?

I used to sleep plenty. It was wonderful all the sleep I got. But now, sleep is not for sale at any cost. I'm counting the days on the calendar. Only seventeen years and fifty weeks before she turns eighteen and moves out of the house.

My mother said, "You'll get used to it. It's a tough job and a big change."

I'll say it is. It's like having an outdoor winter job and showing up the first day in sneakers and a t-shirt. But on the second day, you dress sensibly. The work is still tough, but you are dressed for it.

Here's a better example: A shot of whiskey. First time down the hatch, you're sputtering like an old jalopy. But then, it starts going down smoother. And after awhile, you begin to actually enjoy the taste and the warm feeling.

My mother also says, "Looking into her little face makes you wonder how you ever got along without her." When her face is a wide open scream, nothing but a quivering uvula, I can easily remember how we got along without her. My mom doesn't like that sort of joking. When it comes to the deification of babies, she has no sense of humor. "How about the *defecation* of babies," I said to, unsurprisingly, no appreciative laughter.

Newborn babies have no sense of humor either, but that is part of their charm. In fact, early infancy is the only stage in life when it is acceptable to have no sense of humor. What is normal for an infant is a character flaw in a 30-year-old (and a powder keg in a 15-year-old.) I've noticed this humorlessness in Olivia when she went through the rigors of meeting her other grandmother. My wife's mother is a first-time grandmother and an Italian-American. She kisses Olivia from head to toe to stomach to legs to bum, and then backwards to the head again, twirls her like a baton and misses not an inch of skin with her lips. She performs the baby Manual of Arms. Ten-hut! Mwahh! Twirl! Spin! Mwahh!

Through it all, Olivia's expression remains the same, still and undaunted. She doesn't smile yet. She is like Adam and Eve in the garden, in awe of everything but yet to experience her first joke.

I was holding Olivia and listening to a Spike Jones recording of "Cocktails for Two." I sang along and made all the goofy tromboney and slide whistle noises. I laughed at the absurdity of Spike Jones. My baby, however, saw nothing whatsoever funny about any of it. She started intently at me. There was so much to figure out. Chris Offutt writes about his son, just minutes from the womb, in his book *The Same River Twice.* "It occurred to me he knew mysterious things. What he'd experienced was fresh in his mind, soon to be buried except for nightmares."

So Olivia Rose was not yet capable of laughing at Spike Jones or the Three Stooges or anything. Instead, she wondered what's all this noise and why it eroded her sweet, warm, perfect memories of the womb. Nothing was yet funny to her. Imagine that. There was no absurdity in her world.

I hope she can keep that same expression, that same calm awe and use it to her benefit. If only she could keep her absurdity in check. Yes, there are times when we must laugh at absurd things. We must laugh to survive. But there are other times when absurdity curdles and becomes cynicism. Then it gets in the way of wonder.

Five weeks later, the hurricane is over. It had jolted us, forced us to reflect upon who we are and what it is we value, as if we were examining our property for damage, but in the process we noticed a rose bush we'd never before even seen. I'm not reading as much as I used to, but I do read her face like a book. Her growing cheeks, and not calendars, measure the passage of time.

The Conversation Continues
over coffee and in posts, journals,
books clubs and classrooms.

What gift in your life began as a storm?

*How has parenting changed you? Who were you
then...and who are you now?*

*Think about times when you discovered what you
can and cannot control in life?*

"Reminding us that children are deeper than we think was Charles Schulz's best quality."

Remembrance of Charles Schulz

Just two weeks ago, my six-year-old daughter
Olivia and I were reading from an old
Peanuts cartoon book.

In it, Lucy asked Schroeder:: "You know what
my best quality is?"

"What's quality mean?" Olivia asked me.

"It's a characteristic. Like, what's the best
thing you like about me?"

"I like how you take me to the library," she
said.

"That's my good quality. Now, tell me a bad
quality."

"That's easy," my daughter said. "When you
play that annoying song." She was referring to an
old song, recorded way before both of our times,
Mike Douglas singing the most saccharine of
sentimental numbers, "The Men in My Little Girl's

Life." It's so syrupy she hates it, mainly because I ham it up and sing along. "You know it makes me so mad that I cry," she said. "And you still play it."

"Oh yeah," I said.

Then she got furious. "Don't you know you're not supposed to make little girls cry!" I felt like Schroeder sitting at the piano, getting hollered at by Lucy. That's one of Olivia's best qualities. She shares it with most first-graders. Extreme passion. This is the same little girl who grew sadly solemn one early morning listening to a CD of Mozart flute concertos.

"What's wrong?" I asked.

"The music is making me teary-eyed," she replied.

Reminding us that children are deeper than we think was Charles Schulz's best quality.

In the strip that Olivia and I read, Lucy asked:

"You know what my best quality is?" Lucy answered herself. "I think I'm nice to be around." She paused and added, "I'd hate it if I weren't around."

Well, I'm sure we'll get by, but for awhile I am going to hate it not having Charles Schulz around.

The Conversation Continues
over coffee and in posts, journals, books clubs and classrooms.

Describe a moment with a child that you will always remember.

When has the death of someone famous triggered a personal memory?

What do you think is your best quality? What do people say is your best quality?

"The communicative nature of jazz requires musicians to respond to each other musically on the spot. It is the perfect model for the family dinner. Each one digging what the other has to say, nodding in affirmation. Each one getting his turn."

Give a Little Whistle

In 1992, Bill Clinton told MTV journalist Tabitha Soren that his favorite musician was Thelonius Monk.

"Who's the loneliest monk?" she asked.

I knew just enough about jazz to laugh smugly. I was haughtier than I oughta be. I didn't, for instance, know Monk played piano, let alone play it like no other with splayed finger pecking. I knew that Cannonball Adderly was not one of Gorgeous George's wrestling opponents, but was he a jazz guy or blues guy?

Name recognition is not music appreciation.

My friends thought that Bird played for the Celtics. I knew Bird played a frantic tenor saxophone. Everyone said Charlie Parker was a genius, which I bought, but couldn't say why.

I recently shored up what little I knew by watching every second of *Jazz,* Ken Burns' PBS documentary. It gave me a linear history of the names and their eras, what led to what, who passed torches to whom. I had always recognized the big names and had the good sense to see Wynton Marsalis and Dave Brubeck and others when they came to town. But the jazz documentary helped take my understanding to the next step and I am now, courtesy of the extensive CD collection at the Akron Public Library, exploring more jazz.

And paying it forward.

I showed my seven-year-old daughter Olivia the Benny Goodman portion of the documentary and she loved the fantastic footage of hepcats jitterbugging in zoot suits.

Then we read *Once Upon A Time in Chicago,*

Jonah Winter's fantastic children's book about Benny Goodman. Olivia's storybook concept of royalty now includes a bespectacled King of Swing, and we snapped our fingers to his jumping hits like "Flying Home" and "Clarinet A La King." Later, we watched the portion of the Burns' film examining Miles Davis.

"He plays smooth, cool jazz trumpet," I said.

The next day, I put on the *Kind of Blue* CD and tested my daughter.

"Who is this?"

"Miles Davis," she said.

"What makes you say that?"

"It's quiet and simple. Not fancy like Benny Goodman."

Scootch over, Britney Spears. There's plenty room for all.

In Burns' film, Wynton Marsalis points out

that jazz couldn't be effectively recorded by overdubbing. The communicative nature of jazz requires musicians to respond to each other musically on the spot. It is the perfect model for the family dinner. Each one digging what the other has to say, nodding in affirmation. Each one getting his turn.

Look at the face of someone listening to jazz. That person is *eavesdropping*.

It is a live, in-the-moment form of music, never played the same way twice, lasting as long as it hangs in the air and remains in the memory. The life span of an improvisational riff makes the Monarch butterfly seem like Methuselah.

The writer and philosopher Salvatore Cucchiara says being present – to enjoy jazz riffs, conversations, prayer or even a slice of pizza – allows you to "thrive in the shining now."

That reminds me of my Wright State University literature professor, James Hughes, who taught his students to simply love beautiful things. In a Herman Melville seminar, Hughes opened his copy of *Moby Dick* and read an ornate passage. I wish I could remember which. We English majors, wide-eyed and pale as 60s pop art waifs, hungrily awaited our professor's instruction on what notes to write and why this particular passage gurgled with literary importance. Hughes gently shut the book and smiled.

"Isn't that just wonderful?" he said, leading his factory-farmed sheep to open grazing.

We've all heard that classical music strengthens children's intellects, improves their math abilities. These are fine things, but peripheral benefits to the richest dividend: Music waters the soul.

One early morning before school, my second grade daughter sat on the couch, slowly waking for the day. Softy in the background a CD of Mozart flute concertos played.

"Dad," she said drowsily, "This is making me teary-eyed. It is so beautiful."

That she found it so beautiful moved me too, and she belatedly returned the favor not long after.

We sat idly in the car waiting for a train. While I could not hear above the din, in the rear-view mirror I could see my daughter moving her lips in song. The caboose whizzed by and in the quiet aftermath I listened to her singing "Agnus Dei," *lamb of God* in Latin.

"Beautiful," I said, unaware that she'd even learned it in school. "Would you sing it again?"

In a moment devoid of the self-consciousness that seeps into our media-savvy children like

96

poison, that makes them roll their eyes or mug goofy or shake their booties when all eyes are on them, she sang it again with her eyes closed.

The Conversation Continues
over coffee and in posts, journals, books clubs and
classrooms.

*What have you learned from a child while he or
she was not aware you were observing?*

Who could you listen to all day?

*What thing of beauty – a place, book, song, art,
moment, etc. – do you treasure?*

Dr. Jack Kevorkian (1928-2011) is best known for championing a terminal patient's right to die via physician-assisted suicide; he claimed to have assisted at least 130 patients to that end. He was often known by the nickname "Dr. Death." *The Realist* (1958-2001) was Paul Krassner's pioneering magazine of social-political-religious criticism and satire.

-excerpted from Wikipedia

"Dr. Death Rides Again" appeared in the September, 1994 edition of *The Realist.*

Dr. Death Rides Again

Michigan doctor Jack Kevorkian's assistance in more than two dozen suicides has prompted debate over whether he is playing God. What hasn't been examined, until now, is Kevorkian's influence on the world of free enterprise.

Marty Formby always wanted to open his own business. Kevorkian's philosophy made Marty Formby's dream come true. In his business, *The Gambler's God*, Formby utilizes a painless suicide machine similar to Kevorkian's. Except Formby's patients aren't sick.

"But they *are* scared shitless," Formby says. "Used to be, when a guy gambled himself away up the the eye-teeth, he had to pay up or get an insane loan from a shark. Then he'd have *that* to pay off. It's a no-win situation."

Formby, a former casino card dealer who is

just sixty-six college credits short of a General Studies degree, carefully screens people who have bet, and lost, much more than they can afford.

"It's much easier for them to check out peacefully with me and this machine rather than to face the other music, which ain't so painless if you know what I mean."

Formby, whose business thrives in Atlantic City, is looking to lease office space in Las Vegas and Reno, as well as a mobile euthanasia unit dedicated to Indian reservation gaming sites.

Euthanasians who lack Kevorkian's name recognition often rely on gimmicks to attract clients.

Danny Menning, a Fon du Lac landscaper, used to spend his cold Wisconsin winters collecting meager unemployment checks and unsuccessfully dealing with his unusually long bout of grief over the death of Lucille Ball.

"Like others with extended Lucy grief, I hit lower than bottom. I did a little reading on how to do myself in, learned about this Kevorkian guy, and instead of my ending it all, I mixed in a little American know-how and found a new beginning. Instead of pushing up daisies, I'm rolling in clover!" He spends half the year operating Breath 'n Death, claiming better service than Kevorkian himself.

"I have to. I don't have a medical degree, so I compensate with lower prices. And because I don't have a high school degree, I keep things simple."

Depending on what people can afford, Menning charges up to $5,000 for helping administer his own painless suicide machine ("It's like jumping a battery"), to as little as $25 to assist in guiding a plastic grocery bag over the patient's head, which includes the price of vodka that relaxes the client and encourage cooperation.

Because despair is often preceded by destitution, Menning sells a lot from the $25 menu. Menning adds, "Most rich people I know are happy, which is also good because happy rich folks like nice lawns, especially the full range of landscaping services I offer. But when it comes to real despair, where you wish you wasn't born, poor folks is my bread and butter."

A big surprise is that the Kevorkian debate caused the tobacco industry to reconsider its long-held philosophy. After insisting for three decades that the Surgeon General has been wrong, they now openly admit that smoking is dangerous and often fatal. Spokesman Tony Locust said that the tobacco industry has "turned over a new leaf" and will devote its energy to make the American quality of life better.

And for those whose quality of life is *not* so good? The tobacco industry has adopted a Kevorkian-like goodwill policy that provides a better alternative.

"When we finally decided that smoking was bad," Locust says, "I immediately quit my two-pack-a-day habit. Why? I didn't want to kill myself. I've have a great job, a nice home, a handsome family and a place on the beach. I've got things to live for."

He turns grim. "But not everyone does. Look at our most despondent urban centers or deeply poverty-ridden rural populations. Those kids are born doomed."

Because of this, the tobacco industry promises to distribute cigarettes in America's most troubled communities, the first two years – FREE!

"It doesn't *solve* the problem," Locust explains, "But at least it *initiates* the suicide, even if in slow motion, so that once these kids grow up and see the degradation, the hopelessness, the despair, the imbalanced society that seals them off from opportunity and makes their life a living hell...well, they'll already be dying. That cough, that speck on their lungs, that'll be their ticket to heaven."

But what about those children in these desperate communities who *do* and *will* overcome the odds, gain an education and live fully productive lives?

Locust contends that their early nicotine addictions will be just another one of the many challenges they face – and overcome. "Conquering the cigarette habit will give them yet another accomplishment. These triumphs all contribute to

106

their strong self esteem. We are happy to provide this challenge and no thanks are necessary."

Next in our series: Is Jack Kevorkian obliged to arrange for the kidnapping and assisted suicide of Peter Townshend, a musician who has gone on record as hoping to die before he gets old?

The Conversation Continues

In your observations, how far will people go to justify personal gain?

How has "spin" changed the way business and public service is conducted?

How might this humor piece be considered a tribute to entrepreneurial capitalism?

"I knew there was something wrong with contemporary adults when, as a teenager, I heard parents of young kids piously proclaiming: *Parenting is the toughest job you'll ever love.*"

Grow Up

I just bought a house. Now it is my obligation as an adult to wave the rake handle and holler, "You kids stay off the grass!"

I'm being ironic and I hate that. A few weeks ago I resolved to give up kitsch and irony for the new millennium.

I long for the company of straightforward people who mean what they say and say it without that wink in their voice.

Straight from the shoulders is what I want to be. That's probably why I enjoyed Tom Brokaw's book *The Greatest Generation*, which lauds the men and women who fought World War II. [This essay was published in 2000.]

I grew up in a world shaped by this generation. Most of the adults in my neighborhood were World War II and Korean War veterans or older. Their attitudes trickled down to us. Not only their hand-over-heart reverence for country, which was sorely tested by sixties protest fervor, but simply their hesitance to baby others and themselves. So when one of us pouted on the playground, we would echo our fathers: "Waaahhh! Look who's having a pity party!"

God knows how much self-esteem we blasted right through the growing hole in the ozone layer.

Now that I'm a homeowner, the father of a school-age child, I admire what I saw growing up, and I want to live in a culture that expects me to act my age.

Fat chance.

It wasn't always so. In a recent column, John Rosemond wrote, "Forty years ago, if Frank Sinatra had invited pre-adolescent children over to his house for slumber parties, adults would have been horrified, and when the news got out, that would have been the permanent end of Mr. Sinatra. Today, Michael Jackson, age 35, invites pre-adolescent children to sleep over at his house and the adult community, including the press, who has for more than several years been aware of Jackson's particular affection for children, asks, 'What's the harm?'"

In a 1997 *New Yorker* article, "Kids Are Us," Kurt Anderson writes: "Youth isn't being wasted on the young anymore." The icons of the baby boom generation are now the uninspired subjects of big Hollywood flicks like *Flubber* and *Mr. Magoo.* Video game arcades are likely to be filled with adults, flush with quarters, hogging the machines from fellow customers far less affluent and three decades younger.

"In the early sixties, I would have been

frightened to meet a grownup who read *Fantastic Four* or *Justice League of America*," states Anderson.

In his novel *Wobegon Boy*, Garrison Keillor describes a small town boyhood of the somewhat recent but long-gone past: "Kids migrated around town as free as birds...you were free, but you knew how to behave. You didn't smart off to your elders, and if a lady you didn't know came by and told you to blow your nose, you blew it."

Parents, Keillor continues, didn't "read books about parenting, and when they gathered with other adults, they didn't talk about schools or about prevailing theories of child development. They did not weave their lives around yours. They had their own lives, which were mysterious."

I knew there was something wrong with contemporary adults when, as a teenager, I heard

parents of young kids piously proclaiming:
Parenting is the toughest job you'll ever love.

Take me instead to the world of Charlie in "Death of a Salesman," whose son Bernard went on to a great law career while Biff Loman failed even as, and because, Willy hovered and doted on him.

Willy asks Charlie, "What did you do?"

Charlie says the best thing he did was *not* take an interest. That's my job. Create an environment that's ripe for discovery. Then get out of the way.

The Conversation Continues
over coffee and in posts, journals, books clubs and classrooms.

Has childhood and parenting really changed? Or is this just every generation's complaint, that it was better in the old days?

In your observation, are we unhealthily obsessed with safety – or simply protecting our children?

Do you think children should obey adults the way Garrison Keillor mentions in this essay

"Those like Billy, who can no longer push a broom, remind us why we are here and why we have hearts.."

He Could No Longer Hold a Broom

I had just begun my job as a reporter at a small newspaper located in the county seat. At lunch, the town's restaurants buzzed with clerks, attorneys, politicians, a few reporters and townspeople. It was the kind of community in which a farmer called the judge by his first name because they had played ball together in high school.

At the diner, a frail old man sat on a stool at the counter. Jerry, the restaurant owner and bartender, leaned toward him.

"You want the special, Billy?"

The old man mumbled something. Jerry understood. "Okay, Billy, the ham plate it is."

A few minutes later Jerry set a plate of Salisbury steak before Billy. Billy looked at his plate, puzzled.

"What's wrong, Billy?"

"I...I...wanted ham."

Jerry sighed, wiping his hands on a towel, trying to decide what to do. Lunch was in full swing.

Billy, why don't you just eat this anyway. It's a good special."Then he cut Billy's meat into bite sizes. "There you go, buddy. You eat this and it'll save Nancy from cooking up another lunch.

"Billy shrugged. "Okay. Nancy's busier 'n me."

A few days later in the office, I stepped away from my desk and saw Billy, standing in the doorway wearing worn slippers and old, loose-fitting plaid pajama bottoms. He spotted my notebook and grinned devilishly. "Do you want to interview me?"

What kind of office is this?

A reporter walked by. "Hello, Billy," he said.

Another passed and said nothing. The sight of Billy in pajamas wasn't news. I asked around. An old-timer at the paper leaned back in his chair and smiled. "Oh, you don't know about Billy? He was a janitor here at the newspaper for a long time. Started right when he came back from the war, I think. He retired, but he couldn't stay a stranger very long. He'd come by once a week, grab a cup of coffee, say hi. Stand over our shoulders and backseat drive while we wrote. Then he'd snitch the morning paper and head out. Always left the room singing 'My Wild Irish Rose," like it was his theme song and this was his show. His wife got sick and died and he just got too old to drive. They never had any kids, so he moved next-door. He hangs around town, a sad soul, not his old self. Except when he comes here. Listen...there he goes..."

In the distance we could hear his weak, raspy voice going out the door singing "the sweetest flower that grows..."

"Next door" was a county-run boarding house for the aged and those needing assistance in daily living. Billy often eluded those assigned to help him dress, and he ate lunch at the diner when he had the money, and a lot of times when he didn't. My employer, the publisher of his family-owned newspaper chain, often sat on the stool next to Billy's. They frequently ordered the same lunch special and talked quietly together.

We have a history as a nation of people who build, but in recent years have become less certain. Industries collapse, businesses close, jobs vanish.

We fear that we will be rendered useless in a society that worships vigor and productivity. We feel an empathetic pang when, in *Death of a Salesman*, Willie Loman is fired after decades of service to his firm and cries out "A man is not a piece of fruit!" No one should be disposed of like rind. Too often, however, we discard the rind without seeing how much fruit is left to be tasted. And the taste may be in the satisfaction of continuing to care for that which we mistakenly think is useless.

Those like Billy, who can no longer push a broom, remind us why we are here and why we have hearts. The Billys in our midst give us the privilege, and it *is* a privilege, to live a benevolent life.

The Conversation Continues
over coffee and in posts, journals, books clubs and classrooms.

Why would it be a privilege to live a benevolent life – and not merely an obligation?

The Billys of the world benefit from the kindness of others. Who else benefits?

Who did you think of when you read this essay?

"Eleven rotund men sat around talking, smoking and drinking beer, coffee and sodas. One snored like he was sucking wet carpet through a paper straw. Some were fully dressed Santas. Other were Santa centaurs: half plain old big-boned, big-bellied guy and half Kris Kringle."

Temp Santa

I shop for groceries only because it is preferable to hunting and gathering. While screaming kids and sticky floors give me a headache, it beats skinning rabbits and picking brambles off my sweater...but not by much.

Exception: Grocery shopping is fun in December. You're not standing in gulag soup lines for sundry necessities. You're getting treats! Cinnamon sticks, chestnuts, fresh nutmeg, vanilla beans, chunks of chocolate that resemble coral reef at an oil spill, and of course, Santa likes his Bailey's.

Yes, I shop happily for Christmas groceries, not diapers, butter and detergent, and so I was already feeling cheerful when I spotted a red and green sign on the store's bulletin board: EARN BIG MONEY! ONE NIGHT'S WORK! BRING JOY TO PEOPLE! BE SANTA! I could spread joy *and* earn some dough.

And I needed it. As an adjunct college English instructor, I earned nothing in those weeks between semesters.

Later that afternoon I called the number. Answering machine. On it, a voice about only 25% jolly said, "If yer innarested in being a Santa, then leave your name and a coupla ho-ho's after the beep."

BEEP.

I stammered, "'Twas the night before Christmas and, uh, all through the house, uh, not a creature was stirring...not even a mouse...."

I paused, not sure whether to continue. Then I couldn't remember the next line. So I ended the recitation with an "ummmmmm," took a deep breath and said, "Hgoh-hgoh-hgoh!"

I hadn't cleared my throat and sounded like a chain-smoker at a poker table honking with laughter while cleaning up after a successful bluff.

Three days later I received a call from Mike Swayze, the Santa Broker.

"Can you hold a sec?" he asked, then cupped the phone and hollered at someone, "Either take out the trash or rub my feet. Pick your poison!"

Then to me: "Hey, I liked your ho-ho-ho's. Jolly enough, but I hope you're over the flu. I run a rent-a-Santa operation. People pay me thirty bucks for Santa to come to their house. I give you fifteen. Come to my house at four on Christmas Eve and I'll give you a list of customers and some street maps."

He gave me his address on Hatchet Road, a country lane tucked into the corner of a county that's already so rural that school doesn't start till after the first weekend of deer season.

"That's it?" I asked. "You don't want to see me?"

"You sounded good on the machine," said Mike. "I've been doing this a long time. Trust me, I can tell from a good phone ho-ho."

Those in the biz can leave off the last ho.

"But, Mike, I'm not very round."

"You're probably rounder than you think," he chuckled, a humbling touche. "But hey, don't worry, we got plenty of padding here I can stuff in when we suit you up. Fill up your tank. You'll get twenty bucks for fuel, nothin' for mileage. You'll hit about fifteen houses."

"Fifteen houses?"

"At least. More if I can squeeze 'em in. They'll tip you if you ho-ho good, and if they've been drinking."

I felt queasy. Tidings of discomfort and blecchh, this daunting task of making kids smile. Kids, who 364 days a year are taught to think of clownish strangers as pedophiles. Kids weaned on

130

sitcoms where every character is a corny wise ass
with that smug expression that agrees with the
laugh track, "yes, I AM funny," to these kids, my
ho-ho-ho's are just a misogynist rap lyric.

Oh, how hard could it be. You fling a few
cheap candy canes like Pete Townsend tossing
guitar picks, ask if everyone's been good, then peel
out of the driveway. So what if they don't get a
good look. The secret of Santa is his mystery. My
mother grew up in rural England in the 1930s and
40s. She recalled one prewar Christmas when she
received only two oranges, some nuts and a sack
of treacle candy, but it all remained magical
because she only once or twice fleetingly saw a
real-life Father Christmas and so the true spirit of
Christmas resided in her heart and imagination.

Right then and there I promised to model my
version of Santa after my mother's English
memories. I'd pop my head in the door, wave, then

scoot along, and if I played my cards right I'd earn
some easy cash plus be able to join my wife at her
parents' house by nine o'clock.

"I'll be there," I told Mike Swayze.

"I like to soak my feet in *Epsom* salt!" he
shouted. "This is *table* salt. Like, for my French
fries, not my feet!" Then to me: "Sorry, I got a day
job you don't even wanna hear about. Did you say
you're in?"

Christmas Eve: It took me awhile to find
Hatchet Road. Dusk fell faster than inhibitions at
an office Christmas party. I passed it up four times
thinking it was a farmer's driveway. I searched
local AM stations for weather reports, but instead
heard a heart-tugging hillbilly song about a little
crippled child named Timmy begging his family to
stop arguing about presents and to instead look up
at that great star in the sky. Misty-eyed, I

downshifted the Chevette and pushed down Hatchet Road.

I found the house, up on bricks, at the end of the road by the township's two story pile of road salt. In the yard were nine cars, three with a mottled purple hue, two pickup trucks with rifle racks decorated in red and green lights, a mound of old tractor tires, a faded plywood FIREWORKS FOR SALE sign (the last two letters of SALE squished to fit,) and frozen jeans on the clothesline.

I gulped. This was a trap. All of us schmuck Santas would be bound and gagged in this basement – on Hatchet Road! – while Mike Swayze ran off with our wallets. I slammed the Chevy into reverse. Then came on the radio, "O Holy Night," sung like angels by the South Bronx Blind Kids Choir or the Big Eyed Orphans of Opelika or the Baby Boat People for a Better Way,

I can't quite remember, except that I just turned to boiled mush. I stuffed my wallet under the car seat, trudged to the house and knocked on a screen door that was caked with brown snow. A suspicious old man with a peanut-shaped head *and* torso opened the door and squinted at me.

"Santa?" he grunted.

I was confused. Was I such a natural at this that I was already being mistaken for the jolly old elf even while wearing a pickle green ski parka. "Yes," I said.

"Apartment on the other side of the house," he said and shut the screen door.

I tramped around the house following footsteps that made a narrow path through a foot of snow to an apartment door swung wide open. I followed the sound downstairs to what looked like a combination of theatrical backstage and an eight-day poker game. Eleven rotund men sat around

134

talking, smoking and drinking beer, coffee and sodas. One snored like he was sucking wet carpet through a paper straw. Some were fully dressed Santas. Other were Santa centaurs: half plain old big-boned, big-bellied guy and half Kris Kringle. Behind a card table desk sat the dispatcher of holiday, Jack Webb working the North Pole beat. He didn't rise to greet me. His feet were soaking in a huge sauce pot.

"Mr. Swayze?" I asked.

He stubbed out a Pall Mall and cupped the phone. "*Mister* Swayze? What, is my old man here?" He laughed with a rattle and extended his hand. "I'm Mike? And you are...?"

"Mark Morelli."

He looked me over. "Phew...we *will* be padding you, kid. Do you know Akron?"

"Not really."

"I'll get you a map."

I have many rich images of Christmas: Soft white flakes crossing the beam of light from an iron lamppost...stolen kisses under mistletoe...the crackle of a fireplace..the crunch of snow underfoot while dragging home a tree still dripping sap...me in my rusty Chevette in heavy snowfall, flashlight in my teeth, trying to find a side street on a road map of an unfamiliar town – wait a second!

Was this really the best night to learn the streets of Akron? Driving around in a musty red suit, foam stuffed under my coat, itchy polyester beard. Surely, I'd get lost, arrive late, behind schedule. What if they offered me drinks? I'd be in just the right mood to do some shots, but what about driving? It's not like I'd have reindeer to lead the way.

The fat men doused and lit cigarettes, took leaks and powdered their hair. "Give my houses to someone who knows the city better," I blurted out to Mike Swayze. I was afraid he would tear into me for backing out so late. Instead, he whistled. Everyone grew silent and turned to him.

"Who wants this guy's houses?" Mike said.

The burly men converged like piranha. It was their season, the one time of year when their heft was profitable. The next morning I told my mother about my close brush as a temp Santa. But as I told her about backstage on Hatchet Road, she covered her ears. Sixty-six years old and she still preferred the mystery of Father Christmas, who, like most good things, including the money I wanted that Christmas, was mostly anticipated and rarely seen.

The Conversation Continues
over coffee and in posts, journals,
books clubs and classrooms.

Are there some mysteries of life that are better left alone and unexamined?

What's the weirdest seasonal (or any kind of) job you've ever had?

Discuss when you have said no to an opportunity even though you needed the money.

Uncle Pete's bushes jutted out raggedly, like big gangly green nuclear centipedes. When the wind blew and the branches bristled, Uncle Pete's hedges looked like some foliage cast of *Hair* performing "Aquarius."

The Apostledom of Leaves

My neighbors think I'm lazy because I refuse to rake my leaves. I tell them this: It has nothing to do with laziness. It has to do with my spirituality.

I learned from a very wise and frugal man that by leaving your autumn leaves on the ground, you are expressing the greatest reverence to God. I won't try to control what God has wrought. I won't pretend that I can keep orderly and controlled the perennial fall of His leaves. Let them lie on the ground for a long winter's rest. Let my rakes rust. Thy will be done.

My Uncle Pete taught me this when I was a kid, in the late sixties. Uncle Pete lived across the street, next to Lonnie, who was a whirling dervish of energy who kept busy with his day job in a factory, volunteer fire department, community theater and doing Irish jigs wherever and whenever he could.

When he wasn't working, singing, jigging, acting or fighting fires, Lonnie still had the energy for fastidious yard work. His hedges were carefully contoured, as shapely as a soda bottle. They were in better shape than most American enlistees, which is how Uncle Pete described Lonnie's bushes.

"Look at them, crisp and straight, standing tall at attention. Now look at my bushes, nobody's fools." Uncle Pete's bushes jutted out raggedly, like big gangly green nuclear centipedes. When the wind blew and the branches bristled, Uncle Pete's hedges looked like some foliage cast of *Hair* performing "Aquarius."

"My bushes are expressive. They reach for the sun, they're relaxed, they're letting it all hang out."

Uncle Pete and Lonnie each resembled his own shrubbery. Lonnie stood erect and useful as a shovel. His smile gleamed, like a polished gate. He worked on his yard as if its precision kept us free from Communism. In his military haircut and tucked-in Dickey work shirt, he trimmed and pruned. He scissored his bushes like a surgeon removing a mole.

Uncle Pete was Papa Hemingway in his long white beard and squint-eyed leer with the posture of Groucho. Loose as a goose, he wore jeans with frayed bottoms, swinging and swaying with every step, every little breeze whispering Louise.

He was a tailgunner over China in World War II. He was a little 1950s and a little 1960s. He played scratchy Four Freshmen records in the garage and wore Nehru jackets from Penney's. He let his bushes go so they could find themselves.

"It's respect for God," he said. "You're not trying to put His nature under your thumb, because if you do, it's a losing battle. Everything grows back – grass, beards, leaves – and we're fools to think we control nature." That's when Aunt Lu would pipe in. "He's been saying that since 1953 when we bought this property. Before that we rented and he never had yard work to do. Back then, he talked about the Cleveland Indians and what he wanted on his hamburger. Now every time the leaves turn or the bushes grow, he's the Maharishi."

"Forgive her, Lord," Uncle Pete said groovily. So while the bushes expressed themselves and Aunt Lu raked the leaves, Uncle Pete and I drank root beer in his garage, snapping our fingers to the Four Freshmen, praying for her soul and the soul of Lonnie the Fireman.

The Conversation Continues

over coffee and in posts, journals,
books clubs and classrooms.

Letting the bushes "express themselves" – is that lazy or wise?

What characters in your life did you think of when you read this essay?

Was there a relative or neighbor of a different generation who you would comfortably hang around with?

"Shame on the clergy who don't reserve their harshest judgment for their own sermon writing, who fail to make a good point then just stop, and not go five to fifteen minutes too long. Those tedious, trying extra minutes can often decide whether a soul will deliver Sunday mornings unto God or *Meet the Press.*"

A Child Finds God through His Handiwork Outside of Church

What is church for?

It wasn't a heavy, philosophical question I asked. It was more like a flash card drill.

"To sit still," answered our 3-year-old.

I buckled her into the car seat. "Good," I said. "What else is church for?"

"To sshh," she answered.

"Good," I said, as I pulled out of the driveway. "Church is also for looking at the candles. Church is also for singing along when everyone else is singing. And church is also for watching the priest tell us stories about God. Got it?"

She got it. She promised she got it. Just like she promised last week.

And just like last week, moments after we took our seat in a pew near the front, she squawked and fidgeted. She crawled under the pew. "I want pudding!" echoed all the way to the choir loft.

"This is God's house," I whispered sternly.

"No!" she said. "It's *my* house!"

Theologically, I guess we were both right.

When did it occur to us that the best way to spend a slow-moving autumn Sunday morning would be to force a rambunctious three-year-old to sit still on a hard wooden bench for an event that made watching paint dry seem like a Disney movie.

Children express what adults suppress. And who can blame them? Shame on the clergy who don't reserve their harshest judgment for their own sermon writing, who fail to make a good point then just stop, and not go five to fifteen minutes too long. Those tedious, trying extra minutes can often decide whether a soul will deliver Sunday mornings unto God or *Meet the Press.*

Lively children are to stoic church services what Dean Martin was to apple picking.

Sure, I know, eventually the fidgety kid calms down. She learns about her faith. She becomes a part of something that is bigger than herself, that is so many centuries old that it transcends fad and fashion. She acquires a spiritual identity. She understands what God expects of her and vice versa.

In the meantime, she won't sit still.

Also in the meantime, no one appreciates even that little sip of communion wine more than me.

Midway through the service, I threw in the

towel and took my fussy daughter outside for a walk. I plucked a leaf off a tree and gave it to her.

She smelled the leaf and felt that it was both dry and rubbery. It was green with streaks of red, orange and yellow on the pointed edges. Her fingers traced the borders of the colors.

I thought of how I could teach her why those changing colors indicated that the leaf was dying. I began to speak but stopped.

At that moment, I could see that hers was a divine awe that didn't need a footnote from me, from a priest, from anybody.

Sitting more still than she had been all morning, she gazed at the leaf.

We had left the house that day to witness the God. There, under the tree, we did just that.

The Conversation Continues
over coffee and in posts, journals, books clubs and classrooms.

When and where do you like to pray?

Even though we want the best for our children, how do we sometimes set ourselves up to fail?

Think of times when you realized you don't have control and you let go. What happened?

"The Cold, the Sea and the Stars blessed me with the awesome gift of feeling small and the wisdom that hit TV shows and magazine covers mean nothing more in the big picture than a butterfly's last breath means to you and me."

Going Places, Who Knows Where

I am drawn to both the sea and the river but they both move my mind and heart in different ways.

The sea is like a cat.

It comes in. It goes out. It comes in. It goes out.

The Sea has a day job. The Sea is a commuter. The Sea goes out early but is home for supper. The Sea is Willy Loman.

The River is linear. On occasion it may gush and overflow, but it has direction. It is going places. It is on to bigger things. The River is Willy Loman's brother, Ben. It passes by once in a lifetime and never returns.

"What do you mean, the River never returns? The River is always there!"

That is an illusion. Throw a stick into the

River and it floats away, gone forever. But the Sea is also a dog. Throw a stick into the Sea and the Sea will fetch it and bring it back to you.

Portsmouth, New Hampshire. Its very name connotes two things:

Industry, the port.

And the entrance to a larger body of water.

The mouth of the Piscataqua River in Portsmouth empties into the nearby Atlantic Ocean. When I lived in this beautiful New England town, I spent many hours at the pier in Prescott Park on the edge of the Strawberry Banke, where the first area white settlers came.

On one glorious autumn day I watched walruses flop and frolic in that river. Walruses are sea mammals. They looked like they'd be more at home in stiller waters where they could bob and relax instead of here at a busy part of the

Piscataqua River where the bridge raised and lower when ships came through, where lobster boats sliced through the water each day as if it were an interstate highway. Here it was a salt water river, the Saint Peter's gate of the Piscataqua. It was just miles away from its final destination, the Atlantic, and for all I knew the walruses, like the dolphins men imagined to be mermaids, were the angels that took the spirit of the River and welcomed it to the world of the Sea.

I believe this might be so because the River and the Sea are different.

In the bitter winter, I spent as many hours as I could walking along that New England coastline. The frigid weather and the vastness of the sea joined with the countless stars in the black sky to form Weather, Water and Sky, a ghostly trinity of natural force that enveloped me, intimidated me, and at the same time, delighted me with its ring-around-the-rosey enchantment. The Cold, the Sea and the Stars blessed me with the awesome gift of feeling small and the wisdom that hit TV shows and magazine covers mean nothing more in the big picture than a butterfly's last breath means to you and me.

Hemingway's Old Man faced his sea as the final challenge. Twain's Huck took to his river for freedom. In Viking burials, the dead are shoved out adrift and aflame at sea. It is the end.

But the River churns grist mills. The River makes bread. The River doesn't join hands with any other great ghosts. Unlike the Sea, the River does not cleanse or humble me. The River does not make me feel small.

Most of my time spent looking at rivers has been from bridges in towns and cities, not in nature, so rivers remind me of *human* history. Suspension bridges and smokestacks. Skylines and tunnel entrances. Docks and shipping ports. Sailing and waterfront saloons. If the riverfront industry is long dead, then I see the turned up collars of vagrants and all the other monkey business that keeps the waterfronts busy with unmarked cars and clandestine package drops.

Cities and factories. Restaurants and marinas. Instead of million-miles-away stars twinkling over a black sea. I see winking headlights of cars where couples slouch and swoon.

When my daughters were seven and three, I decided it was time to give them the gift of the Cuyahoga, the river that runs through town. After a year living in Cuyahoga Falls my girls still hadn't come face to face with any wild stretch of the river. I wanted them to feel the energy of the body of water that gave our city its name.

We took a winding road to a park, then hiked down a hillside path till it took us to a part of the river secluded from homes or other buildings. Other than a couple in a passing kayak and an old fellow across the river, we were alone with the Cuyahoga River.

"We're here," I said, gathering stones.

"To do what?" they asked above the loud gushing river.

"This." I pitched stones across the surface.

A half hour later they were still skimming them over the water. I made them little rock piles. None of us spoke. The older one mimicked my sidearm toss and got the hang of it. The little one tossed branches in just to watch them float away.

"There goes another one of my boats," she said.

"Those sticks will float all the way to Cleveland and to Lake Erie," I said. "And who knows where after that!"

"Cool!" said the older one, tossing in a big branch that bobbed in the water before setting course in the current. She was just grasping the fact that it was gone, never to be seen again. I could see her imagining that she touched something that was now going places, who knows where.

The Conversation Continues
over coffee and in posts, journals, books clubs and classrooms.

Describe a moment in nature when you realized
you were part of something vaster?

Think of times when you introduced someone else,
especially a child, to what you consider a natural
wonder.

What body of water – or city skyline or mountain
range or other natural or man-made wonder –
stops you in your tracks?

Mark Morelli is also the author of the short story collection *Tales from Zoalmont and The Melancholy Fringe*, wrote and published the humor 'zine *PAH!* from 1988-2008, and contributed the column "Rearview" to the web magazine *Halfsquare* from 2005-2008. He has been a college teacher, copywriter, reporter, deejay and quiz game writer. He believes even bad coffee can be salvaged by good conversation.

Learn more & view other work at
www.markmorelli.net

continue

the

conversations